Foundatic

MW00718253

The Everyman's Guide to Golf Through Fitness And Strategic Performance

To Wink,

Here's to building your fitness foundation.

A. L. Wilkins

Contents

INTRODUCTION

Foundation – the basis or groundwork of anything; the act of setting up or establishing.

Who is this book for?

First and foremost, ALL golfers can learn something from this book. From the high handicapper who only plays a few rounds a year down to the scratch golfer who plays a few rounds per week. This book will help any golfer get into better shape to physically and strategically perform better in each round of golf that they play.

I can without a doubt say that I love both fitness as well as the game of golf. I've always enjoyed fitness throughout my life but it did not become a passion until much later in life. On the other hand, golf was not even on my radar until I was in my mid-thirties. Yes I had heard of it and knew a few of the rules but I had little or no interest in playing it.

Through my foray into the fitness industry I've gotten to know some great people who have been gracious enough to share with me their love and insights into the game of golf. I quickly became intrigued and began learning everything that I could about the game. This constant appetite has led me to write this book that I believe can assist all golfers in forming their golfing and fitness foundations. Once that foundation is established you will be on your way to becoming more fit and efficient physically and mentally during each and every round of golf that you play.

Uniqueness of Golf

In my lifetime I've played quite a few sports from football to basketball to baseball and a few in between. But none as devilishly challenging as golf. I've always known that in order to become better at most sports that I need to push harder and exert more energy in order to be more successful or simply win. But the game of golf is much more mentally taxing than any sport that I've ever played. Golf is also one of the most counter intuitive activities that I have ever taken part in. You swing easier to make the ball go further. You hit down on the ball to make it go up. And lastly, the lower your score the better you are playing.

In another respect, I believe that building interest in playing golf from any age is quite difficult. You cannot go out and simply pick up a club and ball, gather your friends and get a game started as you could with baseball. You cannot just grab a ball and start making a few shots just like the professionals do as you can during a game of basketball. Also, if you are able to become slightly proficient at swinging a golf club, practicing is such a solitary event that the average person simply can't stand it over a long period of time. The amount of practice time that is needed to become an above average golfer becomes an investment that most golfers cannot or will not make.

Lastly, golf is the only major sport where the equipment changes significantly on a yearly basis. From clubs to balls to shoes, as soon as you buy something just make sure that you understand that a newer/better version of it is soon to follow. Also understand that the same new equipment WILL make you better or at least think you are better. Remember when it comes to determining what to change to improve your game..."It's not the bullets, it's usually the shooter."

Since I cannot change the fact that it seems like golf equipment changes faster than the stock market I plan on giving you a solid fitness and strategic foundation that you can continuously build upon. This doesn't mean that fitness and golfing strategies do not change, but what you will learn within these pages will lead you on a path to becoming a better and well rounded golfer with much improved fitness for not only golf but life.

CHAPTER 1

GOLF FITNESS

Importance of Fitness

The following few pages will delve into some of the most important aspects of the game of golf from the fitness point of view. The sporting world has long since looked to fitness as a way to improve and maintain athletic performance. But it seems as if golf did not really catch on to the importance of fitness until about 15 or so years ago. It used to be looked upon as a bad idea to try to strength train and build muscle while attempting to improve your golf game. It was believed that doing so would inevitably alter your swing in some irreparable way. The belief was that there could not possibly be a way to strength train to become a top notch golfer without looking like a bodybuilder.

But now we are much wiser thanks in large part to many of the younger golfers who have come onto the scene and shown just how beneficial strength training can be. You now see golfers in large numbers touting how adding strength training and conditioning to their daily routines has renewed or extended their golf careers. There is no magic pill that they are using, just simple adherence to a health and fitness protocol on a regular basis. Now it is your turn to find your golf fitness fountain of youth.

The four key ingredients of fitness from a golfing perspective that you NEED to focus on are:

- Flexibility / Mobility
- Balance
- Core Strength
- Endurance

Focusing on the aforementioned elements in a consistent manner will have you well on your way to developing a fitness foundation that can last the rest of your life.

Flexibility / Mobility

Defined: the capacity of a joint or muscle to move through its full range of motion

If I had to choose the most important of the four key ingredients of fitness then flexibility/mobility would be number one. Your ability to move in some parts of your body as well as your ability to stabilize other parts will determine how well you are capable of performing as a golfer. Keep in mind that some golfers are simply blessed with great mobility and flexibility while most golfers will have to work to keep or create it. The following illustration outlines how the human body is set up in an alternate mobility/stability continuum based on its major joints.

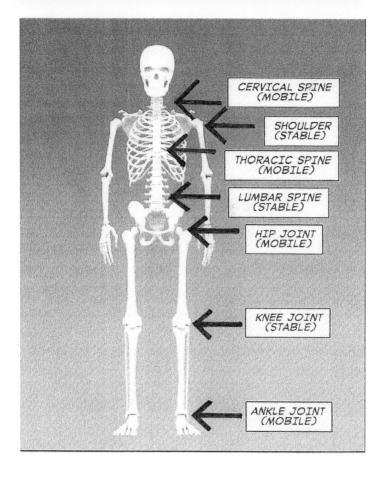

CERVICAL SPINE
(MOBILE)

SHOULDER
(STABLE)

THORACIC SPINE
(MOBILE)

LUMBAR SPINE
(STABLE)

HIP JOINT
(MOBILE)

KNEE JOINT
(STABLE)

ANKLE JOINT
(MOBILE)

The first thing most golfers think of when they hear flexibility or mobility is their ability to turn during their backswing. Although you will need to have good mobility in your thoracic spine in order to make a big turn, you will just as importantly need to have mobility in your hips and ankles to use that big turn effectively.

There are many ways to either maintain or increase your mobility/flexibility. The first method is static stretching which most of us are familiar with from most of the other sports that we've played in our lives. You get into a stretched position and hold it for 20-30 seconds and then move on to the other side or another body part.

The second method is dynamic stretching. This is similar to static stretching but in dynamic stretching you are continuously moving. There is never a time where you will hold a stretch for more than a second or two and then you move on. In dynamic stretching you will also count repetitions where as static stretching is usually done once and then you are finished with that body part. Also, dynamic stretching will work on raising your core temperature as well as waking your central nervous system up. This is all in an effort to get ready for the movements of your intended sport.

The final method is done on a foam roller or a roller of any semi-hard material. The technical term for what you are doing is Self-Myofascial Release or SMR. You are using a foam roller to apply pressure with your own body weight. You simply apply pressure to places that are tender and release the muscle fascia from its 'tightened' state. It is often referred to as the 'poor man's massage' and can be done before physical activity or even as a recovery from your sport.

There are many benefits of SMR as listed below:

- Corrects muscle imbalances
- Improves joint range of motion
- Relieves muscle soreness and joint stress
- Maintains normal functional muscle length

The methods that I've listed are not the only options available to you and I encourage you to find something that works for you. The most important message for you to understand is that you should be doing something to work on your flexibility and mobility. Unfortunately, it is true, if you don't use it you WILL lose it!

Balance

Defined: a state of bodily equilibrium

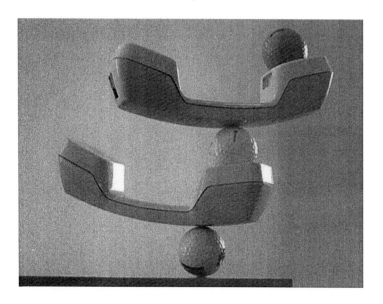

Another important part of any consistently successful golf swing is how balanced the golfer is at all times. You most likely have heard that you must coil and uncoil around your body to create an on plane golf swing. Of course that is a lot easier said than done. From sliding to swaying, golfers use so many swing manifestations as possible to get their club away from and back to the ball in one piece. Having a balanced swing is simply a small part of the equation as inevitably the same golfers will have other physical limitations that contribute to loss of his/her balance.

Even professional golfers are not always in balance as it would be hard to think that the human body could be balanced at all times and especially when we are really looking for it to be balanced the most. The key is to create as stable a platform as you possibly can so when your swing is not as balanced as you would like it to be you can still make consistent contact and play fairly well.

One of the best ways to work on your balance is to use single-legged exercises. They can range from a simple single leg stand for time to a more complex single leg squat. Very seldom in the sporting world are we ever on two legs for an extended period of time and golf is no exception. From shifting your weight to your right leg (right-handed golfer) during your back swing to shifting your weight to your left leg in your follow through, having and maintaining good balance will make both cases much easier.

You can even take balance a step further by adding a dynamic component to your single leg training. Simply move more laterally while completing an exercise and that will force you to quickly adapt to your new positioning just to make sure that you remain standing.

Core Strength

Defined: the strength of the underlying muscles of the torso, which help determine posture.

For quite some time the terms 'core strength' have been at the forefront of the fitness world. But unfortunately when most people hear those words they only think of how strong or defined they can make their abs. Interestingly enough, the core of your body is essentially the entire trunk of your body and it is not only in the front of your body but it works its way all of the way around your body as well. In order to build complete core strength, you will have to use the entire musculature of your core to make it work.

When it comes to golf, there is NOTHING that you do that does not involve your core muscles. As the main support system for your body's physical stability your core is always at work. From its obvious use when you swing a club from beginning to end to sinking a 3-foot putt, your core is always doing its job.

Your core muscles also help you to maintain balance when shifting your body in any direction as well as when you are trying to execute a shot from an awkward lie.

Building core strength is a lot simpler than you may have ever experienced in any gym or even on television. Sadly, most of the world has bought into the idea that if you would like to increase your core strength or get a flatter stomach that you have to do a ridiculous amount of crunches or crunch-like abdominal exercises. This just isn't the case as the crunch the way it is often performed does more harm to your back and very little to your core muscles in the first place.

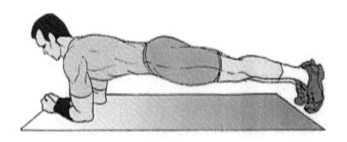

By simply holding the plank position (above) you will work your ENTIRE core musculature while keeping your lower back much safer in the process. Keeping your lower back as safe as possible should be the number one goal for any golfer attempting to increase their core strength through exercise. Finding core exercises in a magazine or on the internet is the easy part. The confusion and injuries come in when the exercises are not applied correctly to the fitness level of anyone trying to do them.

Endurance

Defined: the ability or strength to continue or last, especially despite fatigue, stress, or other adverse conditions; stamina.

When most people hear the word ENDURANCE they immediately think of a picture where someone is running a long distance. Although this is true more often than not, golf endurance is not exactly the same thing. When running you usually begin at a specific point and attempt to maintain your ability to complete your entire trip or distance without stopping. You subsequently begin to build your endurance by completing progressively longer distances each time that you run.

Golf endurance is similar in many ways to running endurance. For starters, the there are defined beginning and ending points in both for the athlete to complete. The goal in golf is always to complete each round at as high an energy level as possible. Runners want to finish each race with as much of a push at the end as possible.

Both sports have defined measures at the end of each that give instant feedback to how well the participant was able to accomplish their task. In golf, finishing the round with a good score is similar to a runner finishing a distance with a good time.

In addition, golf and running both become more mentally challenging the longer you participate in each activity. The longer you run and the more holes you play will take a mental toll on your performance. You ability to remain focused for the duration will greatly improve your overall outcome each time.

The one major difference between running and golf is the amount of cardiovascular exertion exhibited during the two sports. Running any distance will inevitably stress your cardiovascular system on a consistent basis. The game of golf on the other hand will come nowhere close to reaching the same amount of consistent cardiovascular exertion.

Nutrition

Defined: a process in animals and plants involving the intake of nutrient materials and their subsequent assimilation into the tissues.

Just as in any sport that you may compete in, how you feed your body before during and after will greatly determine your success. Unfortunately most average golfers do not pay much attention to how to actually get this done. More often than not a round of golf is as much about having a few rounds of drinks as it is about trying to outdrive their buddies. I am of the opinion that if I am going to pay my heard earned money and spend four plus hours on the course I want to at least play as well as I possibly can.

Now in order to do this there are some simple rules that anyone can follow to make sure that your in-round consumption stays on track.

1. Drink plenty of water before and during your round to stay hydrated
   a. Sports drinks are acceptable if water is not available
2. Have a good pre-round meal with plenty of protein to fuel your body during the round
3. Bring easily packed snacks (nuts, dried/fresh fruit, jerky). Eating these throughout your round will keep your body properly fueled

As you see from the list, healthy options during a round are definitely within your reach and do not take much planning to pull off. In a pinch, grabbing a sandwich from the clubhouse grille can be an alternative but try to stay away from the chips and candies that are often on display.

If you truly are out on the golf course to get better then I would do my best to stay away from ALL alcoholic beverages. I know that so many people partake but in the end they do more harm than good when trying to last an entire round of golf and play well. Especially when the weather is hot, the alcohol will immediately dehydrate and fatigue you making you sluggish from your first beer. And for the record, alcohol does not loosen up your game! Just your wallet loosens up when you are paying your friends for all of the bets that you lost during the round.

Golf Injuries

Defined: harm or damage that is done or sustained

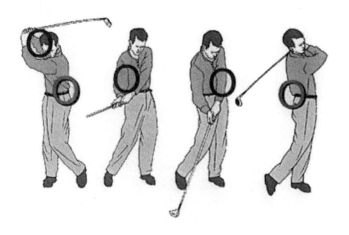

The occurrence of golf related injuries is unavoidable at some point in a golfer's lifetime. Here are a few reasons why average golfers become injured in the first place:

- Average golfers have no pre-round or pre-practice warm-up or stretching routine
- Average golfers have various pre-existing postural limitations due to sedentary lifestyles or work conditions
- Average golfers may have poor swing mechanics based around body limitations which are not addressed through professional instruction
- Average golfers generally do no other physical exercise outside of playing golf

Golfers can get injured in many ways but here is a list of the most commonly seen golfing injuries:

Elbow

Golfer's elbow injuries are a common problem and are similar to tennis elbow, because it is the inflammation of the elbow joint, muscles and tendons close to the elbow. Golfer's elbow or medial epicondylitis is usually on the inside of the elbow where tennis elbow is most commonly felt on the outside of the elbow.

The problem develops because of overuse of this part of the body. The average golfer generally swings a golf club anywhere from 80 to 100 times during a round of golf. This count does not take into account the several times you swing a club during warm up as well. The repetition can also stress the elbow and gripping a golf club the wrong way can also damage the elbow when it is swung. The elbow can become painful and stiff, with making a fist an especially painful act. The hands of a golfer may also begin to feel weak in a player experiencing golfer's elbow.

Shoulder

By far the most common golf injury that affects the shoulder is a rotator cuff injury. The wear that a golfer's swing puts on the set of muscles associated with the shoulder and its socket can tear them as well as tendons, precipitating scar tissue which can impair movement. Arthritis, bursitis and other inflammatory conditions can occur in the joint. In rare instances a golfer can even dislocate his or her shoulder.

Back

Probably the most common health problems faced by golfers are back problems. Almost 36% of the injuries golfers reported were back injuries. There are two factors that make the back the most commonly injured area of a golfer's body. The first is the motion of his or her golf swing while the other is the fact that golfers employ putting stances in which they are often hunched over. Both of these actions put undue strain on any golfer's entire spine.

More specifically, stress from the repetition of a golf swing can also impact the lumbar spine. Weekend warrior golfers are even more susceptible as they are more likely to use more swings in any given round. The mindless bending over used to retrieve the golf ball, pick up clubs or golf bags, and replace divots also contributes to back injuries. Lastly, back arthritis is common in those that golf frequently as it can plague the worn out vertebrate and result in chronic pain.

Wrist/Hand

The wrist action that a golfer uses, as well as the impact of hitting the ball with a golf club, places a lot of stress and pressure on the wrist and hands. When golfers hit the ball, the impact travels through the club and is absorbed by the hands and wrists. As the strokes mount up, they can lead to hand and wrist injury. Tendons can be strained and eventually lose their mobility.

Tendinitis, a stiffness and swelling of a joint, can occur as can carpal tunnel syndrome, a numb feeling that radiates from the wrist to the fingers. Pain in a golfer's hands can be brought about by hard to detect fractures of certain bones that result from striking the ball over and over.

Knees

A golfer's swing can contribute to or worsen a knee injury. Symptoms such as the knee clicking when the golfer walks, pain located in the knee, and swelling that gets worse when the knee is used are common.

Hips can also sometimes be injured by golfers, although this is not a frequently seen injury. The continuous internal and external rotation of the hips will place pressure on both hip sockets. However, existing hip problems can be exacerbated by golfing and a golfer may potentially do even more harm as each round of wear adds up.

While playing the game of golf injuries are bound to occur. There are simple guidelines that you can follow that can either decrease the incidence of injuries or help you to recover from them much faster. The following pre-round warm-up is a great way to get your body ready to swing a golf club. Whether you are playing in your club championship or simply getting in some range time, being physically prepared will allow you to perform at your best from your very first swing.

Pre-Round Warm-Up

1) High Kicks
(x 10each side)

- Start by standing tall with your feet together
- By keeping both of your legs as straight as possible, raise one leg as high as you can while simultaneously reaching out toward that leg with your opposite hand
- DO NOT bend at the waist in order to reach down to touch your foot
- The goal is to remain as 'tall' as possible even if you cannot touch your foot each time
- Complete one side before moving on to the other side

2) Heel to Butt
(x 10each side)

- Start by standing tall with your feet together
- Bring one foot up behind you by bending at the knee and grab that foot with the hand on the same side of your body
- Hold that foot for a two count and release
- Alternate sides until you complete the entire set
- DO NOT lean forward after grabbing your foot as your goal is to remain standing as tall as possible at all times

3) Half Kneeling Overhead Thoracic Rotations
(x 10each side)

- Start in a one knee down/one knee up position (half-kneeling using your golf towel under your knee if necessary)
- Hold your Driver directly over your head with both hands and your arms in a 'Y' position
- While maintaining a tall position through your entire spine, rotate in toward the knee that is up and hold for a 2 count then rotate away from the up knee and hold for a 2 count (that is 1 repetition)

4) Overhead Squats
(x 10)

- Hold your Driver directly over your head with both hands and your arms in a 'Y' position
- Squat down by pushing your hips backward while trying to keep the golf club directly over your head
- If you cannot squat and keep your club directly over your head you can simply hold it in front of your chest to complete your squats

1

1a

2

2a

5) Standing Hip Stretch/Cradle
(2 x 20 seconds each side)

- Start by holding an iron in one hand with the clubhead resting on the ground. You can also hold onto the side of your golf cart if necessary
- Take the opposite leg and rest your ankle across the knee of the leg on the same side that the club is located
- Sit back as far as you can while maintaining your balance thus stretching the hip of the leg that you are no longer standing on

6) Leaning Lat Stretch
(2 x 20 seconds)

- Start by holding an iron with both hands open flat on top of the grip side with the clubhead resting on the ground
- Step back and lean forward by hinging at your hips until your torso is parallel to the ground thus stretching your lat muscles
- Keep in mind that you DO NOT need to put a great deal of pressure down on your club and risk breaking it

1

1a

7) Two Handed Club Rotations
(x 10)

- Start by holding any club with two hands just slightly wider than your shoulders along the shaft of the club
- Take a golf stance
- Next, perform your complete golf swing while keeping your hands in the same place on the club from take-away through follow-through

8) Reverse Club Swings
(Speed creation with club head in hands) (x 20)

- Start by holding your club (Driver) by the clubhead end with your hands on the shaft
- Take your normal golf stance
- Swing the club as you would normally making sure that you hear the "swoosh" at the bottom of your swing

CHAPTER 2

YOU TALKIN' ABOUT PRACTICE?

The Range

For most golfers practicing is the least favorite part of the entire game. This being the case, they often go about it as if it were a chore with no real purpose at all. Many of us have heard that we should 'practice with a purpose'. But what does that really mean? Well, to most of us that usually means that I am heading to the range to PRACTICE with the PURPOSE of getting better. Nobody I know goes to the range to blow money on golf balls to do anything but get better. Unfortunately there is not much getting better in the way that most of us practice. Even though it may seem like a small thing, arriving at the range with a plan is a much better proposition than simply showing up hoping to hit the ball well.

As a general rule, you should practice EXACTLY how you plan to play. You should not just hit the same club until you get it right as the chances of you actually doing the same thing during a round are slim to none. You should start with the picture of a specific hole in mind and determine how you would play that hole even though you are on the range. Hit your tee shot. Hit your approach shot. Maybe hit a shot from just off of the green as if you did not reach the green in two shots. Then repeat that process for a variety of holes as this will get you into the mind frame of dealing with the varying holes on any given course.

I am not saying that you should abandon ever practicing with one club (i.e. Driver) as some days you may feel like you just need to get back into a grove from the tee box. Just keep in mind that you may also need to get off of the tee box with a club other than your Driver so make sure to practice that too. Just make sure that this kind of practice isn't the only reason why you showed up at the range.

Another method of practice that I am in favor of is simply showing up to the range with only the wedges that you would normally use from about 30 yards and in. Just take this time to work on your short game as I am sure that you've heard that that is where most amateurs can make up the most strokes in any given round. Chipping, pitching, your bunker game, as well as your putting become extremely important if/when you are not hitting greens in regulation.

Lessons

Over the years I've had my fair share of golf lessons. Taking golf lessons are just like taking any other type of instructional course because it has to work for you in many ways in order to be successful. Here are a few of the factors to take into account:

- *Instructor* – You may have a friend who has or is currently taking lessons and loves his/her teacher. They rave about how what they are being taught is the best ever and there is no other golf instructor that comes close. Unfortunately this does not mean that the same instructor will work wonders with your game as well. The instructor that you choose needs to work for you and only YOU. You have to be able to constructively work together to determine the best plan for you. If the instructor is trying to teach you something that you are not interested in learning based solely on what he/she thinks is best then that may not work for you. At the same time, if you are not open to learning new things about not only your game but golf in general then you may not be ready to learn from ANYBODY.

- **_Location_** – Where you take your golf lessons is just as important as from whom you get them. You may belong to a country club and prefer to stay in a more comfortable environment to receive your lessons. But you may prefer to go outside of your club or to a private facility to get instruction. Some golfers like having a more focused environment, free from the distraction of other golfers while many have no problem being in the thick of other golfers on the range. Find what works for you and go with it.

- **_Information Intake Speed_** – Simply put, we all learn at different speeds. You may like your instructor to give you numerous lessons with your instruction time for you to work on with no problem. At the same time, you may be the type of golfer who only wants to work on one thing at a time so you can try to master that before moving on. No matter what type of learner you are just be sure to make this known to your instructor.

- **_Dedication_** – Lessons ONLY work if you are going to practice the things that you learn between lessons. It took me quite a few lessons to figure this out but if you learn a new concept or swing thought then it is in your best interest to drive that point home by repeating it as much as possible before your next lesson. Also, you will probably learn things that are different than what you were doing before you decided to take lessons. When you go to practice on your own you will not just pick them up immediately. You will most likely have the urge to go back to what you thought was working before since the 'new' stuff doesn't seem to be working. It will take not only time but dedication and belief in what you are going to accomplish long term for you to see a permanent change.

Training Aids

There are a wide range of training aids on the market that are designed to help you with just about EVERY part of your golf game. I will not attempt to get into them all but I will introduce you to a few that have helped me the most. They may not work as well for you but I encourage you to do your own research to determine which if any training aids you should add to your arsenal.

Optishot Infrared Golf Simulator
(www.optishotgolf.com)

This is the ONE product that helped me the most in my quest to seriously improve my golf game. You may have heard of the Optishot before but if you haven't feel free to visit the website above and check it out. When I was really getting into golf and decided to dedicate myself to getting better I wanted to be able to practice on a regular basis without having to always go to the range. I started researching indoor simulators and found that I did not have the space (no basement) or the funds to actually make it happen.

I stumbled across the Optishot and was intrigued by the price as well as the small amount of space that I would need to get set up. With a small investment for the simulator, a laptop (I wanted a computer dedicated to the Optishot), golf mat and hitting net I was in business. Here is the link to what my actual set up looks like in my garage:

http://northpointfitness.com/pimp-my-garage-optishot-indoor-golf-simulator/

Once I had my simulator set up I was able to customize the software to match my actual club set and was off to play my first round. Over the course of exactly 1 year I went from a 22.5 handicap index down to a 12.5 handicap index. Now I will not be foolish enough to say that Optishot was solely responsible for my improvement as I did play just over 50 rounds of golf in that same time period. But I will say that Optishot was responsible for helping me to develop a repeatable swing that I could work on EVERY day since I never had to worry about the weather.

Tour Sticks (www.toursticks.com)

I use Tour Sticks to this very day. I keep them in my bag for whenever I swing a golf club. From practice days on the range to my pre-round warm-up, I always use them. I cannot exactly quantify how much they have helped me but I will say that they are an excellent way to keep your alignment on track at all times. Whether you are using them to work on perfecting a new swing thought or simply honing in on what you already have been doing well they fit the bill.

Bushnell Laser Rangefinders
(http://www.bushnellgolf.com/laser/laser_rangefinders. cfm)

I use a Bushnell Laser Rangefinder in a couple of ways. First and foremost, I use it during EVERY round of golf to get distances to various points on the golf course. But even just as importantly I use it when I am practicing at the range and need to know distances to numerous points. How many times have you gotten to an unknown range or even your home range and you are not exactly sure how far a flag is? Even though they are usually marked, the practice tees may be in a different location making the posted distances null and void. It is always great to know that I can easily find the correct distance at the press of a button.

CHAPTER 3

GOLFING STRATEGICALLY

Strategy - A plan, method, or series of maneuvers or stratagems for obtaining a specific goal or result.

The definition of the word strategy is so simple yet it is probably so foreign to most of the golfers who set out to play each day. The average golfer pays a fair amount for a round, practices little, but finds it very easy to become upset when their play is below average at best. Unfortunately they were doomed to fail well before they even laced up their golf shoes for the round.

We have strategies for how we plan to accomplish tasks in our everyday professions and they actually pay us for showing up. It would seem that we would be more inclined to have a plan of action for how we would like to play our round of golf especially since we are paying for and hoping to enjoy the round.

Without getting too complicated, I am going to give you a few ideas on how you can make your next round not only more enjoyable but you can actually start setting benchmarks for how your game will improve in the future.

To Tee or not to Tee

Choosing the appropriate tee box

Once you've finished your pre-round warm-up and practice and are ready to tee off it is time to make the decision that will set the tone for your round. You must choose a set of tees to play from and hopefully you put more thought into doing so than the fact that your fellow golfers are playing from the same tees. We've all played with friends or even strangers and feel as if we need to play from the set of tees that they are playing from in order to not look inferior. Sometimes this works but the fact that you didn't use any other means of selecting the tees probably means that they may not be right for your true skill level.

Just because you paid for your round like everyone else doesn't mean that you should tee it up from their tee box just so you fit in. First, you will slow the round down for yourself, the others in your group and most likely the groups that follow you.

Second, you will be in a bad mental position from the start if you know that you are reaching past the level of your game if you know that you are playing from tees that you should not be playing from in the first place.

Lastly, you are golfing to have fun and enjoy your round. The chances of you actually enjoying the round from tees that are too far are very slim at best.

There has been a recent push by the major golfing associations toward a national structure on how to select a set of tees to play call **Tee It Forward**[1]. (See Insert)

Tee It Forward	
Driver Distance	Recommended 18 Hole Yardages
PGA Tour Pro	7600 – 7900
300	7150 – 7400
275	6700 – 6900
250	6200 – 6400
225	5800 – 6000
200	5200 – 5400
175	4400 – 4600
150	3500 – 3700
125	2800 – 3000
100	2100 – 2300

This initiative is aimed at helping golfers choose a set of tees that will allow them to enjoy their round of golf from a yardage that best suits their current skill level. It is also designed to speed the game up for everyone thus keeping the pace of play at an acceptable level. **Tee It Forward** takes your average Driver carry distance into account and suggests corresponding total course yardages that should roughly match your game. This tee selection method is a great idea but in order for it to have a positive effect golfers not only need to know their average Driver carry distance but be brave enough to apply it properly to the chart at all times.

Before this system came about I would select my tee set based on the length of the par 3s on the course. I know that if all of the par 3s in a specific tee set average more than about 185 yards then that tee set is generally too far for me to play from. Another useful method of determining which tee box to choose depends on the distance of the various par 5s on the course. In a general sense, after a good drive into the fairway you should have a reasonable chance to reach the green in two shots in order for that set of tees to work. Now there will definitely be times where you play par 5s that are three shot holes but that should be the exception and not the rule.

You also have to take into account how familiar you are with a course. If you are new to the course, it is a very good idea to play one tee set lower than you normally would due to the fact that you do not have any 'local knowledge' about the course. The last thing you need for your confidence is to hit what you thought was a great shot only to find out that the fairway runs out a little earlier than you thought causing your ball to end up out of bounds.

The bottom line is that no matter which tee set you choose to play from, just make sure that it fits your game and your game only. Swallow your pride, put your ego back in your bag and pick a set of tees that work for your skill level of golf or lack thereof.

Establishing a Pre-Round Game Plan

Scoring

Hole	Black	Gold	Blue	White	Red	Par	+/-	Handicap	Hole	Black	Gold	Blue	White	Red	Par	+/-	Handicap
1	426	414	408	395	329	4		7	10	512	493	485	465	421	5		6
2	212	182	161	135	102	3		17	11	192	178	172	166	138	3		18
3	390	383	361	325	319	4		11	12	391	376	368	345	319	4		12
4	440	423	413	403	345	4		3	13	476	400	395	376	319	4		10
5	559	547	540	526	473	5		9	14	441	429	422	396	365	4		4
6	213	164	149	135	91	3		15	15	525	496	470	458	414	5		8
7	434	419	408	397	333	4		1	16	480	461	416	385	381	4		2
8	407	355	322	304	275	4		13	17	455	401	369	332	267	4		14
9	589	551	532	512	444	5		5	18	232	211	199	168	110	3		16
Out	3670	3438	3294	3132	2711	36			In	3704	3445	3296	3091	2734	36		

Date _____

Scorer _____

Attest _____

Tot	7374	6883	6590	6223	5445	72		
Rating	76.0	73.9	72.6	70.8	72.5		HDCP	
Slope	142	136	133	128	131		NET	

As an amateur golfer you are constantly bombarded with scoring. Whether it is while playing a round with your buddies or while watching a golf tournament on television, the score is always on the top of your mind. When you begin your round, you are handed a score card. When you hear golfers talk about rounds they've played they ALWAYS refer to their score. Lastly, when you drive or walk up to each hole you are more often than not greeted by a sign that tells you what you are EXPECTED to score on that hole if you want to be average.

A few suggestions that I have are to play a round where you do one of two things:

1. You start each hole by adding one stroke to each hole and making that the 'new' par for that hole. Par 3s now become Par4s, Par 4s now become Par 5s and Par 5s now become Par 6s.

2. You play each hole with their normal par but you subtract a stroke after you finish each hole to determine your score. (Bogey = Par, Par = Birdie, Birdie = Eagle)

Each of the above methods does not have to be shared with your playing partners but they are designed to decrease any tension that you may have from the tee box of each hole. They are also designed to help you build confidence across your game overall.

Performance/Scoring Goal Setting

Outside of altering how you score your round you can also set goals to attempt to achieve during each round that you play. You can start with this simple goal progression:

- No Quadruple Bogeys for 9 holes
- No Quadruple Bogeys for 18 holes
- No Triple Bogeys for 9 holes
- No Triple Bogeys for 18 holes
- No Double Bogeys for 9 holes
- No Double Bogeys for 18 holes

If you can accomplish each of these goals there is no way that your overall game will not improve. As scores and your game improve you can begin to add even more specific goals to each round as follows:

- Score par or better on front nine Par 3s
- Score par or better on all Par 3s for a round
- Par or better on at least 3 Par 4s on the front nine
- Par or better on at least 6 Par 4s for a round
- Score par or better on front nine Par 5s
- Score par or better on all Par 5s for a round

As you can see, the goals have become much more specific as the list grows. At the same time, your game will be improving since the goals should be set in a progression where you cannot move on to the next one until the previous goal has been accomplished. You can just as easily set goals within a round or for the entirety of a round. You should definitely start simple when setting these goals because you do not want your sole reason for playing a round of golf to be based on achieving one of these goals.

Here are a few scoring based goals to get you started:

- No 3 putts
- Do not lose more than 3 balls in a round
- Do not lose a ball the entire nine holes/round

Lastly, you can set goals that are purely based on scoring per round and even your overall handicap. That can go as follows:

- Break 50 for 9 holes
- Break 45 for 9 holes
- Break 40 for 9 holes
- Break 100 for 18 holes
- Break 95 for 18 holes
- Break 90 for 18 holes
- Break 85 for 18 holes
- Break 80 for 18 holes

The general idea behind setting and hopefully accomplishing any goal that you set is to build your confidence to play the game of golf as well as to make you an overall better golfer.

The Anatomy of a Golf Shot

The game of golf is unique in that each shot that you take requires the same amount of focus and planning as the previous shot. Bombing a drive down the center of the fairway is soon forgotten if you put your next shot into the water. Knowing this, you should take the same approach to each shot that will put you in the best position for success each time. The method that I like to employ is called **A. I. M.**

A – Assess…the situation

I – Investigate…your options

M – Make…a decision

ASSESS…the situation

Before each golf shot you are faced with numerous tangible factors that need to be taken into account in order to play that shot. These factors include but are not limited to:

- Lie
  - o Fairway
  - o Rough
  - o Sand
  - o Uphill
  - o Downhill
  - o Side Hill

- Wind Conditions
  - o Right to left
  - o Left to right
  - o Down wind
  - o Into the wind

Each of these factors not only affects your club selection but they also affect how confident you will be in even attempting your shot at all. The most commonly assessed factor by all golfers is the lie of the ball. The lie will usually set your confidence level in figuring out what your next shot will be. If you hit a tee shot which you thought was on the right side of the fairway but when you arrived at the ball you notice that it had gone off into the deep rough that immediately decreases the confidence with which you have to make a good second shot. The same can be said in reverse if you thought you had found the bunker on a shot only to discover that you are only in the short rough. Here are a few lie conditions that you will encounter that will shape how you play your next shot:

Fairway – Obviously the most desirable lie condition for you to play your next shot. Ending up in the fairway means that you did something right on your previous shot. By total accident or done on purpose is inconsequential to getting the ball onto the optimal playing surface.

First Cut of Rough – Even though you are just off of the fairway you still have a pretty decent lie to work with. You can play your next shot with the confidence that you will still be able to make solid contact.

Deep Rough – It is not the worst place to end up but you now have to alter your next shot accordingly. Depending upon how gnarly this particular style of rough is you may have to simply focus on getting your ball safely back to the fairway for a much better chance to get to the green. Sometimes you will be lucky enough to play on a course where even the deep rough is not much of a hazard and you can still get pretty solid contact on your next shot.

Sand Bunker – Depending upon how your ball ended up in the bunker your next shot can vary between slightly different shot all the way to damage control shot. If you are in damage control you should simply take your medicine, get your ball back to a better lie and try not to get back into that position again.

Misc. (Pine straw/Woods) – If you find yourself here it means that you've strayed off of the course just a bit but you can still find your ball. Rarely will you have an open shot toward the green but more often than not you will be forced to punch a shot back out into the fairway.

Once you've determined what the lie of the ball is you can then start adding in other factors which will help you decide what to do next.

The next most commonly ascertained factor is the distance from your ball to the hole. This number can and will often mislead amateur golfers who consistently look for a distance to a point that they should probably never even think about. Most of the time amateur golfers would be much better served and would also score better it they take aim at the center of the green.

Now that you have the distance to your intended target you can determine whether or not the wind will have any affect on your shot. You will also have to determine how high or low the green is in relation to your location. After taking in all of your pre-shot factors you can now select the club that you plan to use to make your next shot. But before you swing the club you still have to move through the next progression of investigating your shot options.

INVESTIGATE...your options

When investigating your options you will now have to determine how the course is set up and if that will have an affect on your proposed shot. Here are a few key factors to consider:

- Hazards
    - on the right
    - on the left
    - to carry
    - to lay up in front of

- Out of Bounds location
- Realistic distance to the green

While investigating your options you are often faced with two main questions that will need to be answered before playing each shot that will hopefully keep you on track to shooting good scores. Those questions are:

1. What can I realistically accomplish with my next shot?
2. If I do miss my intended target, where is the best place to do so?

It may seem like an odd thing to consider but knowing whether or not you can hit the ball safely to the actual distance that you measured will definitely guide the remainder of your decision process. For instance, if you are 235 yards from the center of the green can you realistically reach the green on your next shot? For most amateurs the answer is probably in the range of about 1 out of every 10 attempts or less. Knowing that, you can immediately begin to look for an appropriate lay up distance with a club that you are much more confident in hitting.

You will also have to take into account how wide or narrow of a landing area that you will have for your approach or next shot. Knowing this bit of information can help you avoid aiming your shot toward an area of the course that makes it highly likely that you will end up in an undesirable location. We would all like to be able to stick all of our approach shots to within three feet of the hole but the reality is that we will rarely do so. Even if we do pull it off it will be more the result of circumstance than planning and actual technique.

You may think that choosing where you would like to miss is inviting negative thoughts into your head. The truth is that even professional golfers do not hit each shot perfectly and getting away with a miss-hit is often a product of proper planning and not dumb luck. If you ask yourself these two questions before each shot, you will inevitably put yourself in positions where you can consistently score well.

Lastly, are there any hazards to consider for your next shot? Do you need to avoid a steep drop-off on the right side of the green? Do you need to clear two bunkers fronting the green? Do you need your next shot to carry a small creek in order to safely make it to the next landing area?

All of these questions are not only valid but will guide you down the correct path through club selection and shot attempt. Just like most other golfers, my goal on a large number of my shots is to land the ball in as safe a place as possible. Doing so requires you to always keep the fact that you are playing against the course in your mind. This approach is similar to when you hear a football commentator say "taking what the defense gives you." The course will never give you the same conditions from round to round. You will also not hit each shot the same no matter how often you play the same course. Your objective is to determine what the course is giving you on any given day and process that information through the filter of what you would like to get accomplished.

MAKE...a decision

This seems like the easiest step to complete because all of the information has been processed. I would argue that this is in fact the HARDEST step of all to complete. It is the hardest step due to the fact that all forms of doubt will begin to seep into your mind as to whether you can actually do what you told yourself that you could get done. Your club has been chosen and you know where you plan on landing the ball but what if something goes wrong?

Have you played a similar shot in the recent past and that negative outcome now makes you weary of having a repeat performance? Will the wind kick up just as you take the club away thus disturbing your focus? Will a noise from a playing partner or just from the surrounding area disrupt your swing enough to throw you off line?

Making a decision becomes the hardest step to complete only if you do not fully commit to the decision that you've made. This is not the same as backing away from a shot as the wind kicks up or stepping away to read your putting line again. Not committing forces you to stand over the ball long enough to let not only doubt seep into your head but tension into your entire body.

The first way to increase your level of commitment in your next shot is to have the right club in your hand to begin with. How many times have you walked away from your cart/bag and down to your ball only to realize that you have the wrong club in your hand? Instead of heading back to the cart/bag to get the correct club you simply try to make your previous selection 'work' which inevitably does not. Solve this problem by taking enough clubs with you from the start just in case a shot factor changes so that you can be ready for it.

What I believe is the best way to increase your level of commitment is to have a reliable pre-shot routine that you NEVER stray from. This routine can be whatever you would like it to be but it should have the following characteristics:

1. *Repeatability* – Your routine should be basic enough that you can actually remember it.

2. *Simple* – the routine should be straight to the point where it does not take too long to get done. Even if you back away from a shot and start over it should still be concise enough to be performed again without creating a delay for others.

3. *Relaxing* – the whole point of the routine is to get you into a position to freely swing the golf club and achieve your desired result.

No matter what your pre-shot routine is going to be you should keep it consistent while on the course. If you decide to change it between rounds that is up to you but while on the course DO NOT change it in any way. The course, conditions and playing partners will be enough of a distraction to you that you need at least one thing to bring you back to some measure of consistency.

Golfing From Green to Tee

Putting

Unlike how you would actually play a golf hole, we are going to begin with the end of the hole in mind. Outside of a hole-in-one, holing out on your approach or simply chipping in, your putter is the one club in your bag that you will use on every hole.

If you ever take notice whenever you are at your local driving range you will see that a vast majority of golfers will show up and immediately begin to hit balls with every club except their putter. You would think that since it is the most active club in your bag that it would get the most work but that simply is not the case. It just isn't as sexy to roll putts as it is to blast a long drive or to try to stick an iron shot to within feet of a far away flag stick.

When it comes to putting, I cannot tell you that there is a more accepted method for getting it done than anything else but I do know that it is something that you have to 'feel' in order to become consistent. From the style of the putter to the length of the putter shaft, what works for one golfer to the next is simply a matter of taste and what they feel is working for them at the time. Putters are often treated like starting quarterbacks. If the one your are using right now does not seem to be working for whatever reason just put the back up in play and see if you get better results. I personally own at least three putters at any given time and have switched them from round to round because the fact that one is not working could never be me.

At the same time, the style of putting that you use is again something that you must get comfortable with and then practice until it becomes repeatable. This also goes for reading greens to determine the line and speed of your putt. You should have a general method that you employ on a regular basis but since greens are different from course to course, you will have to learn to adapt pretty quickly.

It is a no-brainer that any time that your ball is on the green that you will be putting as your next shot. Most of the time you will be trying to actually sink the putt but what if you are sitting 75 feet from the hole? Yes, draining that miracle putt would be something you can tell your grandchildren but how realistic is it? Would it not be a better idea to lag that long putt up near the hole leaving yourself a nice little second putt instead of trying to make the long putt and either leaving it very short or blasting it by the hole? In this case it was easy to determine what club to hit but just as or even more importantly determining how to play the shot is what matters much more.

Now what if instead of being on the green you are on the fringe or just past the fringe? You are now faced with the decision of whether to chip or putt the next shot. Well, the more consistent shot for most amateurs is to putt the ball to get it rolling as soon as possible which you can control a lot easier than a chip shot. Now sometimes the fringe is just too thick or you may be more comfortable chipping in which case you should choose the shot that you feel that you can most confidently execute.

Bunker Play

During many golf broadcasts you will hear the announcer say that the pro would much rather have his or her golf ball land in the bunker than another place on the course is due to the fact that professional golfers are like artists when it comes to playing bunker shots and can pretty much make the ball do what they want it to do. On the other hand, most amateurs are deathly afraid of hitting out of any sand bunker.

First things first, all sand bunkers are not created equal. Even though they cause concern for most golfers myself included, they are not to be feared as hazards that cannot be conquered. For starters, you have fairway bunkers and you have greenside bunkers. Within those two categories the size and depth of bunker will vary from course to course. Lastly, the consistency of the sand in each bunker will vary and sometimes within bunkers on the same golf course.

Many times, simply getting out of the bunker to begin with is the most that you can hope for in order to play your next shot from a more suitable lie. Other times, you will have more options and be able to do more when getting the ball out of the bunker. If playing out of sand bunkers still makes you nervous then your best bet would be to get out of the bunker in as few strokes as possible. If not, your score will balloon before you can even reach the green. No matter how often you find yourself in any sand bunker you will definitely have to employ the A. I. M. system to find the best solution to getting yourself back on track.

Tee Shots

From my personal experience to the experiences of my fellow amateur playing partners, getting safely off of the tee box is paramount to scoring well in any round of golf. You will often watch professional golfers hit into the woods or into deep rough and still make par or bogey at worse. An amateur can hope to make bogey but more often than not their score ends up as double-bogey or higher.

We all know what it feels like to hit a tee shot into the water or out of bounds and have to hit another tee shot and keep the next one safe. The thought of laying three or even five is enough to get into anyone's head. That is why it is so important to have a go-to shot or club from the tee box to keep you in play on as many holes as possible. Even though it may seem unpopular among my playing partners I've often hit a long iron off of the tee of a par five if I know I would not attempt to get to the green in two shots with the best drive I've ever hit. The idea behind it is to simply minimize as much risk as possible. If I can more consistently get into the fairway at about 220 yards I can easily get home in two more shots thus avoiding any trouble from the tee box with my less accurate driver.

If you have a go-to shot or club it will also decrease the amount of stress that you feel when teeing off throughout your round. Even if you are forced to play for bogey from the tee box to avoid trouble off of the tee you will start the hole knowing that you will avoid double or even triple-bogey by being conservative from the start. The bottom line, get into the fairway consistently and good things will happen.

General Rules for each Type of Golf Hole

There are only three types of holes on any golf course, Par 3, Par 4 and Par 5s. The number and layout of each type will vary from course to course but you will most likely get a chance to play each type a few times per round.

Par 3s

The par 3 hole is generally the easiest of the holes on the golf course. You get one shot to get the ball onto the green and in rare cases you may even hit your tee shot directly into the hole for a hole-in-one. You can even specifically practice these shots from varying distances when on any driving range to get better at them.

At the same time, these holes can become some of the toughest on the course if they are very long, are guarded by sand bunkers or water, have huge changes in elevation or have undulating green complexes. There are usually 3-4 par 3s on any given 18-hole course so you will have numerous opportunities to score well on them. There are also par 3 or executive courses made up entirely of par 3s. Playing one of these courses affords you a great opportunity to work on your par 3 strategy under 'live' conditions.

The key to being consistently successful on par 3s is to make sure that you are eliminating as much risk as possible when playing them. Getting par on a par 3 is a good score and being able to do so consistently will definitely keep your scores low. My basic point of strategy is to always aim for the center of the green no matter how tempting it may be to do otherwise. I would much rather hit the center of the green and take my chances making two putts and even three at worse than to try to hit a well guarded pin and find myself in a ton of trouble. Also, this center of the green mentality will lead to a birdie from time to time but more importantly it will also help to keep you from blowing up on a hole or even the entire round.

Par 4s

Par 4 holes are under most circumstances the most plentiful on any golf course. They can range from very short and less challenging to very long and extremely challenging and anywhere in between.

The most important aspect of playing any par 4 is to determine how you want to play it from the tee box. Having a solid plan of attack will give you realistic expectations for what is about to take place over your next few shots. You may get up to a par 4 and from the tee box you know for sure that you will not even need to hit your driver and can safely get into the fairway with a middle to long iron. There will also be times when even if you do hit your driver that you should play the hole with a score of bogey being as good as a par. This usually happens when a hole is simply too long or playing much longer than you comfortably hit the golf ball. In this case, it is much wiser to play this par 4 as a par 5 and hopefully you can take your bogey and move on to the next hole.

Par 5s

The par 5 hole to me is the most interesting hole on the golf course as the risk/reward scenario often comes into play big time. For starters and just like the par 3s you will see anywhere from 2-4 par 5s on any given golf course. But that is where the similarities end. Par 5s can sometimes be so short that it makes you feel as if you are playing a par 4. On the other hand, there are some par 5s that make it a struggle to get home in three shots.

When most golfers come upon a par 5 they immediately reach for their driver since they know that par 5s are usually the longest holes on the course. They would be much better served to 'play' the hole from green back to the tee in their mind to make a final decision as to what club to take from the tee box. If you know for a fact that you cannot or will not reach the green in two shots then it may be in your best interest to hit a short and more accurate club off of the tee.

You can get safely into the fairway with a shorter club, play your second shot a good distance closer to the hole and then hit the green in regulation with your third shot. But I do understand that you are often playing with your buddies and since they are hitting drivers then you simply have to as well or at least you feel pressured to do so. Unfortunately, they don't have to share your score at the end of the round so keep that in mind.

At the same time, hitting a long and well placed tee shot can turn that par 5 into a long par 4 so to speak where a birdie is in your immediate future and who wouldn't want that?

Finishing the round strong

Golf has always come under of fire when it comes to determining whether it is simply a recreational game or an actual sport. In most professional sports, the men and women playing them are in peak physical condition in order to be at the top of their respective games. Professional golfers on the other hand have been widely criticized for not at least looking like they care about their physical condition in order to play.

But over the past few decades, golfers of all skill levels have become more aware of what physical conditioning can do for themselves as well as their games. Here are a few of the many ways that golfers have become more active:

- Strength Training
- Flexibility Training
- Balance Training
- Cardiovascular Training

Now keep in mind that the four training methods listed above DO NOT need to be treated as four separate entities. Many times they are paired or even all combined into a single method of training.

Regular exercise has given golfers the ability to not only play better but to also play longer. It has allowed many golfers to quickly recover from round to round as well as to recover from any injury they may suffer through continued play. No matter how you decide to train the point is that you do something. Golf IS a sport and you will need to be able to compete physically from hole number 1 through hole number 18. Even though you are not running like football or basketball your body is still being asked to perform a full body movement a large number of times over a long period of time. In order to stay 'fresh' on the 18th hole as you were on the 1st you will have to train your body to be that way.

19ᵗʰ *Hole*

This section will get into many of the ancillary aspects of the game of golf. Outside of the main equipment most often associated with playing a round of golf, there are a multitude of products that are said to be able to help your entire game improve.

Establishing a handicap

A golf handicap is a numerical measure of a golfer's potential playing ability based on the tees played for a given course. It is used to calculate a net score from the number of strokes actually played during a competition, thus allowing players of different proficiency to play against each other on somewhat equal terms. The higher the handicap of a player, the poorer the player is relative to those with lower handicaps.

A handicap is calculated with a specific arithmetic formula that approximates how many strokes above or below par a player might be able to play, because it's based on his or her ten best scores. A player's handicap is intended to show a player's potential, not his average score, as is the common belief. Handicap systems are generally based on calculating an individual player's playing ability from his recent history of rounds. Therefore, a handicap is not fixed but is regularly adjusted to increases or decreases in a player's scoring.

In the United States, handicaps are calculated using several variables: The player's scores from his most recent rounds, and the course rating and slope from those rounds. A "handicap differential" is calculated from the scores, using the course slope and rating, and the player's handicap differentials are used to calculate the player's handicap.

The most respected resource for maintaining a golf handicap in the United States is a USGA (United States Golf Association) system called GHIN (Golf Handicap and Information Network) at www.ghin.com. If you are just learning the game of golf then establishing a handicap may not need to be high on your list of priorities. But as your game progresses and you are beginning to play more then having an established handicap will only enhance your consistent improvement. Also, if you are ever interested in playing in any competitive rounds you will undoubtedly need to have an officially established handicap.

Laser Range Finders & GPS Devices

We all want to play our best golf each time that we tee it up for a round. In order to do so we base most of our decisions in golf on the distance our ball currently sits from a number of landmarks. Although many courses have been marked with distances from a few places on each hole, they may not be places that you find to be convenient or even accurate enough for you.

With this in mind, many golfers have taken it upon themselves to use devices during a round that will make finding accurate distances to objects on the course from anywhere much easier. They usually take the form of either GPS tracking units or laser range finders.

The GPS tracking unit uses a satellite based system to determine your position on the course/hole relative to various other landmarks on the course/hole. Most of the top of the line GPS units are pretty accurate to within a yard of the actual distance you are looking for. They can be used on thousands of courses all over the world and some can even keep your score for the round.

The downside of GPS is that it does require a clear satellite signal to be effective so that can be a problem from time to time. You may also have to manually download courses to your device before each round in order to have the most recently updated information.

There are also laser range finders that can be used to determine your distance to points on any course. They are simple point and shoot devices that easily measure from where you are standing to exactly where your laser locks on to. They are pretty accurate for hundreds of yards and to within a yard of the actual distance as well. They can be used anywhere in the world without ever having to make sure specific course information is loaded on them.

The drawbacks of using a laser are that you usually need a pretty steady hand to get the laser to lock on to your exact target. Also, you can only measure the distance to objects that you can lock on to. For example, if the green is located behind a large hill that blocks your view you obviously cannot lock in on the flag as it is hidden from your view. Lastly, laser range finders do not have the ability to track your score or any other in-round information.

Score Tracking

During every round that you play you are given a score card by the course to record your scores for each hole that you play. But getting better at the game of golf is much more involved than simply knowing what your final score was during a given round. The following questions can be asked after each round:

- Was I hitting fairways in regulation consistently?
- Was I hitting greens in regulation consistently?
- Did I have any three-putts?
- How well did I play out of the sand?
- How well did I recover or scramble?
- Were my club distances consistent?

All of the above questions and many more can be answered by keeping more detailed accounts of each round that you play. Even though it may sound complicated to do, the process of tracking this information is quite easy. There are a large number of applications for smart phones that easily allow you to enter this information between shots or at the end of each hole without interrupting your round. Here are a few examples:

- Golfshot: Golf GPS
- Golfsites – Golf GPS with ball tracking & rangefinder
- GolfCard GPS
- GolfCard GPS+
- Fun Golf GPS with 3D maps

Having instant feedback upon completion of each round as to what you did well along with what you need to improve on is invaluable.

CHAPTER 4

Let's Tee It Up

This entire chapter will be devoted to "playing" an entire round of golf from a strategic perspective. Each hole will be broken down from tee to green and a few hypothetical twists will be added to force numerous decisions to be made to finish the hole. The round will be played from a tee set measuring about 6100 total yards. We will also make the assumption that you were a mid/high handicapper trying to establish consistency across all levels of your game.

Hole #1 (Par 5 – 505 Yards)

You need to take Driver from the tee box in order to reach the fairway. There is a hill on the left kicking tee shots into it back into the fairway but there is also a reachable bunker on the right. A really good drive gives you the option of going for the green in two but a drive to the right even if not in the bunker forces you to lay up with your next shot.

Assuming that you are in the fairway the next shot should be a layup to just inside of the 150 yard mark. Now that you are inside of 150 yards planning your approach shot is next. The green is fronted by a bunker and there is also a bunker behind the green making controlling your distance pretty important. There is water in front of and to the right of the green. The safest play is to aim toward the left center of the green no matter where the pin is placed that day. This strategy takes as much trouble out of the equation as possible while still giving you a decent play toward a good score.

You are now on the fringe on the left side of the green and even though you are 35 feet from the hole, you've avoided the hazards. The fringe is cut short enough for you to putt so you finish out the hole in three more shots for bogey. Not a bad start!

Hole #2 (Par 3 – 132 Yards)

       This short par 3 is surrounded by three bunkers, one front right and the other two behind the green. Although water will be in your eye line, it should not come into play unless you completely miss-hit your tee shot short and left. Regardless of where the flag is located you should use yardage to the middle of the green to select your club off of the tee. You should aim toward the center of the green as a safe place to hopefully land as well.

       Your tee shot lands in the middle of the green just as you planned it. You take two putts to finish the hole for par. Nice!

Hole #3 (Par 4 – 354 Yards)

This is a dogleg right par 4 that goes slightly uphill as you approach the green. You can take Driver here unless you have a club that you can more accurately hit about 200 yards. If you can get a club into the fairway at around 200 yards you will be left with just over 150 yards to the center of the green. If you do decide to hit Driver just know that there is a small clearing on the left and you have some forgiveness on the right with a small hill but not too far as you do not want to have your second shot blocked by trees.

You've taken driver and you ended up in the right rough after hitting a slight slice that kicked off of the hill. Your approach shot is partially blocked by trees on the right but you do have a shot at the left side of the green. You have about 145 yards to the green and the only bunker is behind the green on the left hand side.

Due to your tee shot, the trees on the right and the back left bunker are the only obstacles that you need to avoid. Your approach shot doesn't quite reach the green but it at least avoided any trouble. You chip onto the green and finish the hole with two putts for a bogey. Not bad after your slightly errant drive.

Hole #4 (Par 5 – 507 Yards)

Next is a slightly downhill par 5 that is also a dogleg left. Driver is needed off of the tee in order to reach the fairway. The bunkers on the left should be avoided but the hills on the right although not ideal are a much better bailout position.

Your tee shot is one of the best that you've ever hit and runs down the fairway to the top of the hill. You can clearly see the downhill green and you are a little over 250 yards from the center of the green. The chances of you getting to the green in two shots are very slim so I suggest that your next shot be a layup to a comfortable distance. Even though you decided to lay up, you need to avoid going left at all costs as the fairway slopes that way. Also, if you go too far right then your next shot is blocked by trees on the right.

Your next shot goes about 140 yards but it slices right and your view to the green is obstructed by trees. This is one of those times where you should simply take your medicine and play for a safe shot.

You can only see just off of the left side of the green so you hit your wedge into the rough on the left side of the green but you successfully avoided any of the three greenside bunkers. You chip on and finish the hole in two putts for a bogey. Good recovery and nice job avoiding a big number by going for a hero shot.

Hole #5 (Par 4 – 356 Yards)

This is a relatively straight par 4 with a slight uphill tee shot. You do not need to hit your Driver off of the tee and you will be much better served by hitting your more accurate 200 yard shot to the top of the hill. The left side of the fairway is not only lined with bunkers but if you miss the bunkers, your tee shot will run down the hill and out of bounds. The right side is much more forgiving if your tee shot strays there.

Your tee shot ends up slicing right but not drastically and you end up just off of the fairway. Now that you are on the right side of the fairway the front greenside bunkers are much more in play as you attempt to hit the green on your next shot. Take enough club to carry the bunkers as going long is much less of a penalty than coming up short.

Your next shot unfortunately ends up in one of the front greenside bunkers after a thinned approach shot. Your next concern should simply be to get out of

the bunker and onto the green and not trying to hole
your bunker shot.

You get out of the bunker and onto the green
in one shot but you three putt for double bogey.

The next hole is a pretty short dogleg right par 4. Again, Driver is not needed so go back to that 200 yard club that you can get into the fairway more regularly. There are bunkers on the left side of the fairway but you will not be able to reach them with less than Driver off of the tee. The only real danger is the water that runs down the right side of the fairway and will only come into play if you slice your tee shot so aim a little more left if needed.

You hit your tee shot and after aiming left to avoid the water you hit the dreaded straight ball but it still ended up in the fairway but on the left side. Your approach shot is a little longer than you wanted it to be but it is still only about 145 yards to the center of the green.

Even though this hole is pretty short, the green is guarded by three bunkers. The water will still be in play with a slice so staying left is not the worst idea. Your approach shot is hit fat and your ball although safe ends up about 10 yards off of the front of the green.

You chip onto the green and finish the hole in two putts for a bogey. At least you avoided any hazards.

Hole #7 (Par 4 – 331 Yards)

Again, this is another short par 4 that doglegs a little more to the left. It is also downhill so even though you do not need to hit your Driver, you can hit even less than your 200 yard club as you simply need to get past the cluster of trees on the left which are about 180 yards away. You can simply pick a club between 200 and 180 yards that you are most comfortable with and put it into play. Even though you can see a bunker in the distance it will not be in play with the correct club selection off of the tee.

Your tee shot finds the fairway and gets past the trees on the left putting you in great position for your approach shot. You have about 135 yards to the middle of the green but there are bunkers in the front and the back of the green that you would like to avoid.

Your approach shot makes the green and ends up within 12 feet of the cup. You two putt for par and take that confidence to the next tee box.

Hole #8 (Par 3 – 150 Yards)

Here you have an uphill par 3 that is heavily guarded by greenside bunkers. The distance posted to the center of the green from the tee box is 150 yards but the hole will play one club longer. Given a choice, going right is a better miss than going left off of the tee as the fairway slopes off drastically on the left side. Lastly, you want to make sure that you take enough club to clear the bunkers in the front and at least get to the green.

You hit your tee shot fat and it doesn't even reach the bunkers. Although not impossible, you are now faced with an uphill pitch shot that must clear the bunkers to get to the green. It is time to 'take your medicine' and just put the ball on the green with your next shot and take your chances with your putting.

You pitch your next shot onto the green and finish out the hole in two putts for bogey. As intimidating as this hole can be that is not a bad score.

Hole #9 (Par 4 – 338 Yards)

This is a pretty straight ahead par 4 but unfortunately the green cannot be seen from the tee box. The hole is not very long but it is paramount that you get your tee shot to the top of the hill in order to have an open shot into the green. Once again you should ditch the Driver and hit your more consistent 200 yard club to the top of the hill.

Straight is definitely the best option but missing to the right is much more forgiving than missing to the left.

Your tee shot is perfectly placed at the top of the hill where you are 150 yards away from a downhill two tiered green. Of course you would like to get your approach shot onto the correct tier of the green but getting onto the green at all is much more important. The only hazards to navigate are the three greenside bunkers and being a little long is safe miss.

Your approach shot lands right in the middle of the green but rolls down to the lower tier of the green. The cup is on the upper tier which gives you a fit and you finish the hole in three putts for bogey.

The back nine starts with a straightforward par 3 which plays a little longer than the listed yardage. The green is pretty well flanked by bunkers leaving the right side as your only bailout area. Just make sure not to go too far right as the trees can come into play with a shot that slices far right.

You end up hitting your tee shot flush and with the extra club it ends up in the bunker behind the green. You get your next shot out of the bunker but a little too far as it rolls into the bunker in front of the green. Your next shot finally reaches the green and you two putt for double bogey. Not the best way to start the back nine but you need to recover mentally for the next tee shot.

Hole #11 (Par 4 – 366 Yards)

This hole is a downhill par 4 that doglegs right to an elevated green. You can take Driver off of the tee making sure to get around the corner to have a shot at the green. Going right is not out of bounds but it forces you to pitch back out into the fairway especially if you reach the bunker. Going left is a better option as the ball will usually kick back into the fairway off of the hill.

Your drive slices slightly right but just to the left of the bunker. You now have a clear approach shot to an elevated green. Make sure to take enough club to get the ball up the hill and safely onto the green. The only bunker is behind the green so you have a pretty clear path as long as you do not go long.

Your approach shot is right on target for the center of the green. You finish the hole in two putts for your third par of the day. Great recovery from last hole!

Hole #12 (Par 4 – 367 Yards)

This par 4 is a bit deceiving. The listed yardage says that it is not too far but since the fairway turns hard right, the tee shot is the first of at least two delicate shots that you will have to play. To reach the hill in the distance is about 220 yards so you will have to again call on your 200 yard club to get you safely into the fairway. The only possible problem from the tee is if you slice the ball into the trees on the right. You will be able to find your ball but you will most likely be pitching back into the fairway to get a shot at the green. If you go left, there is an opening but your shot into the green will be a lot longer than you would like it to be.

Your tee shot is sliced into the trees and you find it about 10 yards off of the fairway in the woods. You pitch your next shot back into the fairway even though there was a small opening. As tempting as it looked, the chances of you actually pulling off the through the trees shot right onto the green were quite small.

Now back in the fairway you have a clear view of the green which is surrounded by trouble. Steep drop-off on two sides and a bunker on the third side make this shot pretty scary. You hit your next shot to the fairway in front of the green as you became tentative with your stroke. You chip on and finish the hole in two putts for double bogey.

Hole #13 (Par 5 – 498 Yards)

The next hole is a dogleg left par 5 where trees crowd your eye line from the tee box. Getting your tee shot into the fairway is of utmost importance on this hole in order to keep moving forward safely. I would take the club that you are most comfortable hitting at least 220 yards to get into the fairway. This will definitely be a three shot par 5 so don't get too greedy off of the tee.

You hit Driver and get the ball safely into the fairway. You can now see the green which is up hill and to the left. Your next shot should be used to try to keep your ball in the fairway and to get ready for your approach shot.

You lay up your next shot on the right side of the fairway and even though the green is to the left, you still have a decent look at the green. Your current angle puts the greenside bunkers on both the right and the left making a straight shot a little more important.

Your approach shot lands short of the green but you are able to chip on and finish the hole in two putts for a bogey.

Hole #14 (Par 4 – 314 Yards)

This is another short par 4 with trouble from tee to green. Driver is definitely not needed unless you are planning on going for the green. A tee shot that goes about 180 yards will do just fine to avoid the bunkers on the right as well as keep your ball from catching the fairway on the left and heading into the woods.

Your tee shot goes right but just past the tree in the distance. You have a shot into the green but coming out of the rough will make carrying the front bunker and avoiding the back bunker much harder. The safer option may be to play to the right to avoid the bunkers all together even though it means not hitting the green.

Your approach shot does go right and you were able to avoid the bunkers. Your pitch shot is thinned and shoots across the green but still not into either bunker. You chip onto the green and finish out in two putts for double bogey. It is time to refocus to keep this round from getting away from you.

Hole #15 (Par 4 – 363 Yards)

The downhill tee shot on this par 4 looks so inviting. From the tee box you see a huge landing area but make sure to take into account the bunkers on the left. The only other danger would be if you go to the right thus blocking out any approaches from that side. You do not need Driver on this hole especially if that 200 yards club is working well. Getting into the fairway at just over 200 yards makes getting to the green so much easier.

Your tee shot lands and runs down the right side of the fairway setting up a good look at the green for your approach shot which goes slightly uphill. There are bunkers in the front and behind the green but the green is large enough to hold most shots.

Your approach shot finds the green and you are able to two putt for a much needed par to get back on track.

Hole #16 (Par 5 – 480 Yards)

Here we have a par 5 that doglegs right. Since you are not going for the green in two shots I suggest that you take the unpopular but much safer tee shot and hit your 200 yard club again. Getting into the fairway safely at 200 yards and still getting to the green in three shots is much easier to do than hoping to get into the fairway with Driver. Plus, the 200 yard club takes all of the potential Driver danger out of play.

Just like the last hole, you hit your 200 yard club well and you are set up for your next shot from the fairway. Your next shot is a lay up to about 120 yards and you are still in the fairway. Your approach shot is now very manageable to a slightly elevated green guarded by just two bunkers in the front.

Your approach shot lands on the back fringe where you can still putt the ball. You lag your first putt to within 3 feet and finish the hole with another putt for par. Two in a row!

Hole #17 (Par 3 – 179 Yards)

The final par 3 on the course is pretty challenging even though it looks quite simple. For starters, it is the longest on the course and there are three bunkers on the sides of the green ready to catch any wayward tee shots.

Take enough club to get you safely to the middle of the green while making a smooth swing. If you happen to come up short you will still be free of trouble and have a straight opening into the green for your pitch shot.

You hit your tee shot a little thin and get about 90% of the way to the green. You are about 10 yards off of the front of the green and ready to pitch on. Your pitch shot ends up not getting onto the green as far as you would like it to have. You are able to two putt to complete the hole with a bogey.

Hole #18 (Par 4 – 379 Yards)

  The very last hole is a par 4 that is pretty straight. The trees on the right give the hole the illusion that it is much narrower than it actually is. Take Driver and make sure that you avoid the hanging branches on the right as well as the bunker on the right as you pass the trees. Missing left is ok as your ball can kick back into the fairway and you are still left with a clear shot into the green.

  Your tee shot goes right but misses the branches on the right. Unfortunately your ball finds its way into the fairway bunker on the right side. This is not the time to try to make the best shot of your round especially if you are not very good out of fairway bunkers. Instead, take a club with enough loft to clear the lip of the bunker if there is one. You simply want to get the ball out of the bunker, advance it a decent distance and not put yourself in any more trouble.

Your next shot gets you out of the bunker and lands about 50 yards in front of the green. You now have a much better approach into the green from a lie that makes you much more comfortable.

Your next shot finds the green and you two putt for your final bogey of the round.

Post Round Summary

Front Nine

The front nine scoring went as follows:

Pars: 2
Bogeys: 6
Double Bogeys: 1

Total Score: 44 (+8)

The front nine was pretty uneventful just like you need it to be to build confidence. The only hiccup was the double bogey on the 5th hole which was due to a poor approach shot that forced you into recovery mode from the sand. You were one stroke better than bogey golf for the front nine which is much better than average on any round of golf.

Back Nine

Pars: 3
Bogeys: 3
Double Bogeys: 3

Total Score: 45 (+9)

Round Score: 89

The back nine was much more of a rollercoaster than the front nine. You made a few more big scores on holes on the back than you did on the front but you had one more par on the back nine. Shooting an 89 is still above average for any amateur so you should be proud of what you were able to do. By working on a few things in your game your scores will get better over time.

CHAPTER 5

SAMPLE WORKOUT

(Always consult your physician before starting any
exercise program)

As a Certified Golf Fitness Instructor I've assessed the movement patterns of hundreds of golfers. In doing so, I've been able to identify a few areas where golfers are consistently deficient. They are:

- Thoracic Spine Flexibility
- Hamstring Flexibility
- Glute Strength
- Core Strength
- General Balance

Here is a simple workout designed to address the inconsistencies and imbalances that I've commonly encountered. Each exercise will be accompanied by a regressed (easier) as well as a progressed (more advanced) exercise.

Lower Body & Balance

Box Bridges
- Floor Bridges (Regressed)
- Single Leg Bridges (Progressed)

Single Leg Reaches
- Single Leg Reaches to Wall (Regressed)
- Resisted (Progressed)

Core Stabilization

Anti-Rotation Circles
- Anti-Rotation Press (Regressed)
- Half-Kneeling Low to High Chops (Progressed)

Plank
- Knees (Regressed)
- Marching Feet (Progressed)

Foam Roller (Complete one set of #1-4, then start back at #1)

1. Thoracic Spine Rolls
2. Thoracic Crunches
3. Quad Crossbody Stretch
4. Lying Thoracic Rotations

Box Bridges
(3 sets of 15 repetitions)

Focus Area:
- Glute Strength
- Hamstring Stabilization
- Low Back Stabilization

Exercise Execution:
- Begin by lying on your back with your heels on a box no more than 12 inches in height
- Lay your arms to your side at a 45 degree angle from your body with your palms up
- Bring both of your feet in as closely as you comfortable can while keeping them on the box
- Bring your forearms off of the ground
- Push through your elbows and your heels to raise you hips off of the ground and squeeze your glutes at the top of the rep while holding for a second at the top
- Return to your starting position for a brief second and then continue into the next repetition until you complete the entire set

Floor Bridges (Regression)
(3 sets of 15 repetitions)

Focus Area:
- Glute Strength
- Hamstring Stabilization
- Low Back Stabilization

Exercise Execution:
- Begin by lying on your back
- Lay your arms to your side at a 45 degree angle from your body with your palms up
- Bring both of your feet in as closely as you comfortably can and raise your toes off of the ground
- Bring your forearms off of the ground
- Push through your elbows and your heels to raise you hips off of the ground and squeeze your glutes at the top of the rep while holding for a second at the top
- Return to your starting position for a brief second and then continue into the next repetition until you complete the entire set

Single Leg Box Bridges (Progression)
(3 sets of 12 repetitions per leg)

Focus Area:
- Glute Strength
- Hamstring Stabilization
- Low Back Stabilization

Exercise Execution:
- Begin by lying on your back with one of your heels on a box no more than 12 inches in height while your other leg is hovering over the box
- Lay your arms to your side at a 45 degree angle from your body with your palms up
- Bring your foot in as closely as you comfortable can while keeping it on the box
- Bring your forearms off of the ground
- Push through your elbows and your heel to raise your hips off of the ground and squeeze your glutes at the top of the rep while holding for a second at the top
- Return to your starting position for a brief second and then continue into the next repetition until you complete the entire set and then switch legs

1

2

Single Leg Reaches
(3 sets of 10 repetitions per leg)

Focus Area:
- Balance
- Glute Strength
- Hamstring Flexibility
- Low Back Stabilization

Exercise Execution:
- Begin by standing tall with your shoulders back and down away from your ears and your arms at your sides
- The main keys to this exercise will be your ability to lead with your chest while simultaneously hinging at your hip joint
- Your legs should start with a slight bend in them
- As you lean your chest forward and hinge at your hip joint, you will also need to raise one leg off of the ground to match the lean in your chest.
- Once your back is parallel to the ground you can return to your starting position
- Complete all reps on one side before moving on to the next leg

Single Leg Reaches to Wall (Regression)
(3 sets of 10 repetitions per leg)

Focus Area:
- Balance
- Glute Strength
- Hamstring Flexibility
- Low Back Stabilization

Exercise Execution:
- Begin by standing tall with your shoulders back and down away from your ears and your arms at your sides
- The main keys to this exercise will be your ability to lead with your chest while simultaneously hinging at your hip joint
- Your legs should start with a slight bend in them
- As you lean chest forward and hinge at your hip joint, you will also need to raise one leg off of the ground to match the lean in your chest while also reaching toward the wall or in this case a tall box
- Once your back is parallel to the ground you can return to your starting position
- The wall/box is there simply for confidence building and to keep you from falling over
- You should aim to get close to the wall but not use it unless you have to
- Complete all reps on one side before moving on to the next leg

Single Leg Deadlifts (Progression)
(3 sets of 10 repetitions per leg)

Focus Area:
- Balance
- Glute Strength
- Hamstring Flexibility
- Low Back Stabilization

Exercise Execution:
- Begin by standing tall with your shoulders back and down away from your ears and your arms to your side while you are holding weights in each hand
- The main keys to this exercise will be your ability to lead with your chest while simultaneously hinging at your hip joint
- Your legs should start with a slight bend in them
- As you lean chest forward and hinge at your hip joint, you will also need to raise one leg off of the ground to match the lean in your chest.
- Once your back is parallel to the ground and your weights are on both sides of your knee you can return to your starting position
- Complete all reps on one side before moving on to the next leg

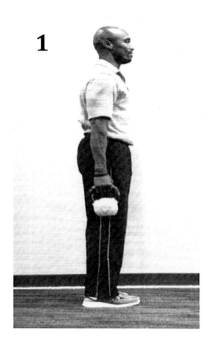

Anti-Rotation Circles
(3 sets of 15 repetitions each side)

Focus Area:
- Core Strength

Exercise Execution:
- You will need to have a resistance band attached to a stable connection attached at about your shoulder height
- Holding the band with both hands, begin by standing tall with your shoulders back and down away from your ears with a slight bend in your knees
- You can raise your arms straight out in front of you to shoulder height
- Choose which direction that you would like to begin and simply make medium sized circles with your hands
- Complete the entire set facing one direction, turn around to switch sides and repeat
- To make the exercise less challenging you can move closer to the band connection and away from the connection to make the exercise more challenging

Anti-Rotation Press (Regression)
(3 sets of 10 repetitions each side)

Focus Area:
- Core Strength

Exercise Execution:
- You will need to have a resistance band attached to a stable connection attached at about your shoulder height
- Holding the band with both hands, begin by standing tall with your shoulders back and down away from your ears with a slight bend in your knees
- You can raise your arms to shoulder height while keeping them 'attached' to your chest
- Begin the exercise by pressing your hands out to straighten your arms thus engaging your core muscles and then back to their starting position
- Complete the entire set facing one direction, switch sides and repeat
- To make the exercise less challenging you can move closer to the band connection and away from the connection to make the exercise more challenging

Half-Kneeling Low to High Chop (Progression)
(3 sets of 10 repetitions each side)

Focus Area:
- Core Strength

Exercise Execution:
- You will need to have a resistance band attached to a stable connection attached at your about ankle height
- You will start the exercise with your inside knee on the ground and your outside knee up
- Holding the band with both hands, begin by 'standing tall' with your shoulders back and down away from your ears and your hands down in front of your inside knee
- Begin the exercise by moving your hands right to the middle of your chest and then immediately out and away from your body in an angled fashion to engage your core muscles. Bring your hands back in front of your chest and then back down to their starting position
- Complete the entire set facing one direction, switch sides and repeat
- To make the exercise less challenging you can move closer to the band connection and away from the connection to make the exercise more challenging. You can also increase the exercise intensity by placing your raised knee more in line with your lower knee

Plank
(3 sets of 20-30 seconds)

Focus Area:
- Core Strength

Exercise Execution:
- Begin by lying on your stomach with your forearms directly under your shoulders
- Start the exercise by flexing your toes on both feet up toward your face while raising your entire body off of the ground
- Your head should be in a neutral position with your legs completely locked and your glutes tight
- Avoid letting your hips drop down thus hyper extending your lower back

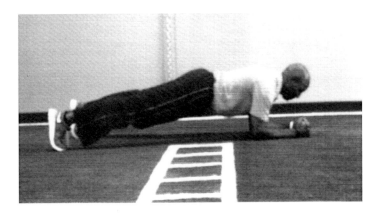

Knee Plank (Regressed)
(3 sets of 20-30 seconds)

Focus Area:
- Core Strength

Exercise Execution:
- Begin by lying on your stomach with your forearms directly under your shoulders
- Start the exercise by engaging your core muscles and raising your body up onto your knees
- Your head should be in a neutral position with your glutes tight
- Avoid letting your hips drop down thus hyper extending your lower back

Marching Plank (Progressed)
(3 sets of 30 seconds)

Focus Area:
- Core Strength

Exercise Execution:
- Begin by lying on your stomach with your forearms directly under your shoulders
- Start the exercise by flexing your toes on both feet up toward your face while raising your entire body off of the ground
- Your head should be in a neutral position with your legs completely locked and your glutes tight
- Once you are in the planked position, alternately raise and lower you feet slightly off of the ground in a marching fashion
- Avoid letting your hips drop down thus hyper extending your lower back

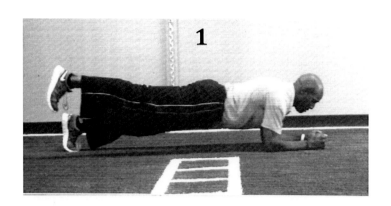

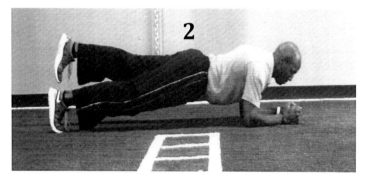

Thoracic Spine Roll
(2 sets of 10 rolls)

Focus Area:
- Thoracic Flexibility

Exercise Execution:
- You will need to have a foam roller available
- Begin by lying on the foam roller as it sits just across your upper back
- Place your hands over your ears in order to have your elbows either touch or get as close together as possible
- Raise your hips off of the ground and roll the foam roller down your upper back to the middle of your back and then return to the top
- Repeat to complete all of the repetitions making sure to NEVER roll your lower back

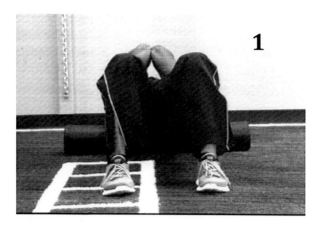

Thoracic Crunches
(2 sets of 10)

Focus Area:
- Thoracic Flexibility

Exercise Execution:
- You will need to have a foam roller available
- Begin by lying on the foam roller with the roller in the upper middle of your back
- Place your hands over your ears in order to have your elbows either touch or get as close together as possible
- While staying seated on the ground and your elbows together, extend back as far as you can to stretch your thoracic spine and then return to your starting position
- Repeat to complete all of the repetitions

1

1a

2

Lying Thoracic Rotations
(2 sets of 10 rotations each side)

Focus Area:
- Thoracic Flexibility

Exercise Execution:
- You will need to have a foam roller available
- Begin by lying directly on your side with your arms straight out in front of you at shoulder height and the foam roller under your head for comfort
- Bring your top knee up as high as you can and make sure that it touches the floor taking it to at least 90 degrees or above thus protecting your lower back
- Take your top arm away from your bottom arm (keeping it straight) to as far as you can open it and then back to start
- Make sure that you are following your hand with your eyes during the rotation
- Make sure that you are also keeping your top knee firmly planted on the ground at all times
- Complete the entire set on one side before moving on to the other side

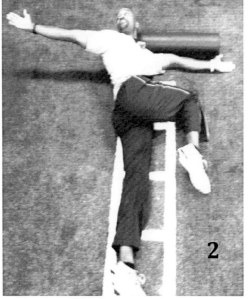

Endnotes

"foundation." *dictionary.com.* 2013.
http://www.dictionary.com (8 March 2013).

"balance." *dictionary.com.* 2013.
http://www.dictionary.com (8 March 2013).

"core strength." *dictionary.com.* 2013.
http://www.dictionary.com (8 March 2013).

"endurance." *dictionary.com.* 2013.
http://www.dictionary.com (8 March 2013).

"nutrition." *dictionary.com.* 2013.
http://www.dictionary.com (8 March 2013).

"injury." *dictionary.com.* 2013.
http://www.dictionary.com (8 March 2013).

"strategy." *dictionary.com.* 2013.
http://www.dictionary.com (8 March 2013).

[1] "Tee It Forward." *pga.com.* 2013. www.pga.com
(29 March 2013).

Acknowledgements

This book is born from my passion for both fitness and golf. With that said, I am hoping that whoever takes the time to read this book is able to take away at least one thing from its contents. With so many golfers of all skill levels taking to the course on a regular basis I am sure that there is something for each of you in this book.

Next I would like to give thanks to each and every client that I've been blessed with the opportunity to train at North Point Fitness in Roswell, GA. I am especially thankful for all of the NPF golfers who were gracious enough to share their ongoing golfing experiences with me. From the rounds that you've played all around the world to allowing me to tag along with you for a round or two, those experiences fueled my passion for the game and this book.

Lastly, I would like to thank any colleague that I have ever had the pleasure of working with at North Point Fitness. Every day has always been a new adventure that my NPF family has travelled right alongside me. I never knew that a group of relative strangers could come together on a regular basis and give so much love. It is here where I've been truly able to enjoy what I do on a regular basis and since coming here I've yet to have to 'work' a single day.